Dedicated to Ethan and Austin...
&
Holiday, Bella and Zatanna.

To teach you how <u>not</u> to pick your nose in public.

The Itchy, Itchy Booger Book is published by Clean Noses and More.

No part of this publication may be reproduced in whole or in part without written permission of the author. For information regarding permission, email: ItchyBoogerBook@gmail.com

ISBN 0-692-70959-2

Here are some tips and tricks

For when your nose gets an itch

To keep you from having to pick.

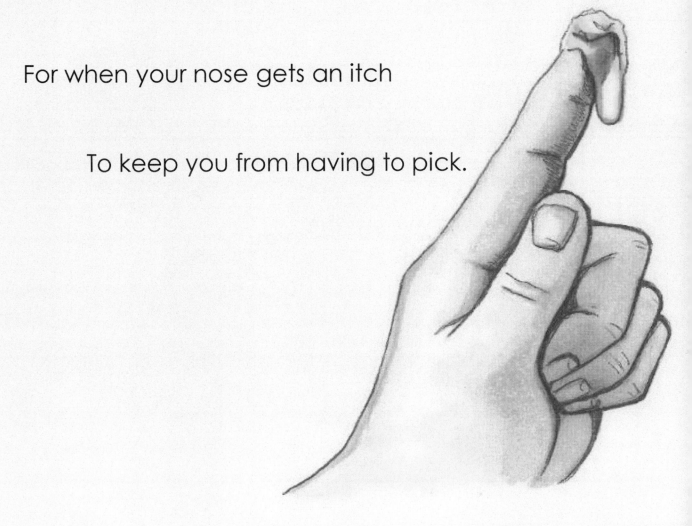

We all know our nose can be icky, sticky and kind of itchy.

Do you think that booger in your nose is a salty treat?

Like a newly discovered piece of meat?

Your nose can run in the spring, summer and fall.

Flowers, grass
and leaves
can make
you sneeze
and a... Aa..
ACHOO!

So let me just say ahead of
time, "God bless YOU!"

Dogs and cats

Dust and rats

Allergies will come...

I can promise that!

Technique #1: Follow the PLAYBOOK!

"Classic, basic and a MUST HAVE when sick!"

Tissues can come in many forms.
Handkerchiefs are cool and should be the norm.

You could use a napkin, toilet paper or a paper towel.

Just don't get flagged in public for a
finger-in-the-nose foul!

"Illegal use of the hands!"

Technique #2: Shoulder-Sleeve Shuffle
"Go-to-move for those facing a tough opponent..."

When no tissue is around or crumbled newspaper to be found don't let your nose drip to the ground!

The shoulder-Sleeve Shuffle will require sleeves, but with practice you can do it with ease.

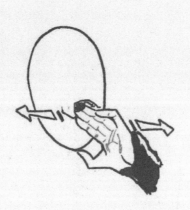

Using the shirt covering your forearm or shoulder,

Especially good when months get colder,

Rub your nose up

and down

to keep from

looking like a

clown.

Technique #3: Undershirt Carry
"Creating a distraction is vital!"

Only really available when your shirt is untucked, but based on how kids dress these days I'm sure you'll be in luck!

If possible, pretend to kneel down to tie your shoes, or if barefoot fake a bad itch – You Choose!

At the same time, grab the bottom of your shirt and fold it inside out to give your nose a much needed clean out.

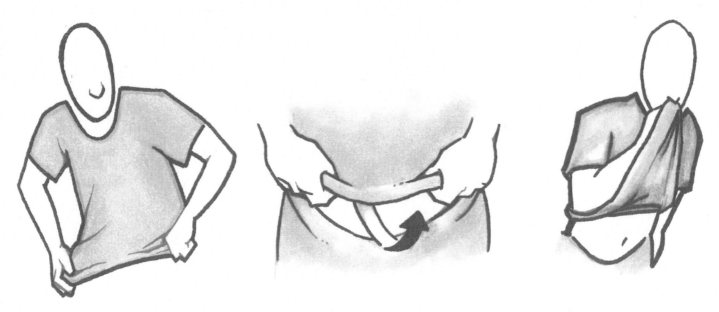

If you can't find a bathroom and these tips don't work

Don't hit the button

Stay Calm

Let's not go BERSERK!!!

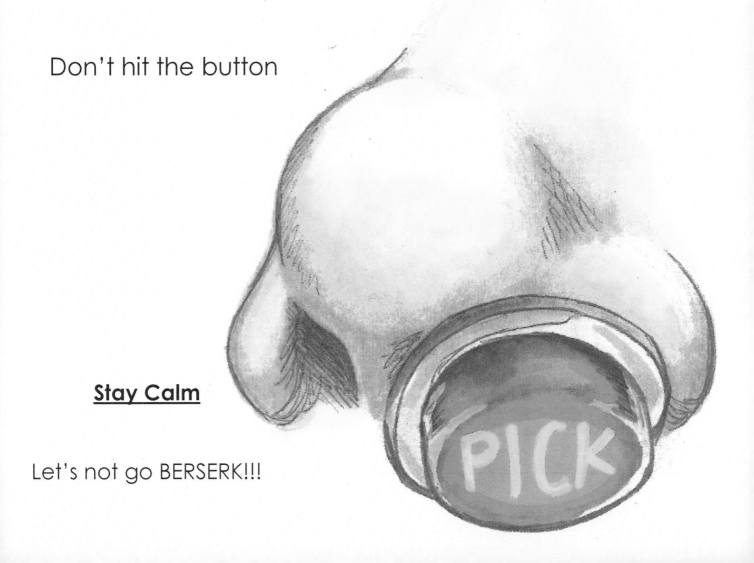

Simply use the last pages of this book...

Boogers go here

And, here...

With room for more boogers

Oops! Time to get a new book!

Or find a tissue, napkin, handkerchief,
paper towel, toilet paper or shirt!

Made in the USA
Lexington, KY
14 July 2018